Spousal Support

In Network Marketing

Donna Fason

insight
PUBLISHING GROUP
Tulsa, Oklahoma

SPOUSAL SUPPORT IN NETWORK MARKETING
© 2005 by Donna Fason

Published by Insight Publishing Group
8801 S. Yale, Suite 410
Tulsa, OK 74137
918-493-1718

ISBN 1-932503-38-2
Library of Congress catalog card number: 2004114333

Printed in the United States of America

Contents

Foreword

I had known Donna Fason for almost two years before she approached me about reading the manuscript she had written called *Spousal Support in Network Marketing*. I could see pride in her eyes regarding her accomplishment and I was flattered that she would ask me to review it and provide comments. I agreed and give thanks each day for my wonderful decision.

My initial reading was in Donna's home state of Arkansas where she and her husband, Robert, live in Mount Vernon with their two children. After a few pages, I couldn't stop. I read until I was finished and forgot I had skipped breakfast and was beyond lunchtime in my hotel. It didn't matter. I was enthralled, interested, and fascinated. I read the manuscript again.

After returning to Atlanta, I began searching book titles and subjects to determine if anything had been written regarding the role of a wife (or husband) in a network marketing business where patience, endurance, and as Donna calls it, "support," had been explained in a useful, how-to-do-it book. I could find nothing. In fact, the literature in network marketing, to be fair, is redundant. There are literally dozens upon dozens of books simply rehashing the same theme. In other words, I long ago found little or no originality in the area, with the possible exception of the monumental *Network Marketing* written by Dr. Keith Lagos. (Dr. Lagos is a respected author who has written the only textbook on network marketing and is also the publisher of *Moneymaker's Monthly* and one of the stalwarts in the Direct Selling Association).

I remained amazed and elated. Donna Fason, I concluded, had written an original book in network marketing that I knew beyond any doubt would be popular with both wives and husbands who would benefit by her sharing of experiences. And, I might add, her experiences are profound. Her story of struggle that she and Robert have endured to elevate their family through economic success is an invigorating, admirable saga of the American Dream realized. Robert would be the first to tell anyone that his own remarkable success would not have happened without the creative support, patience, faith, and endurance of Donna. You may be absolutely certain that the Fason's have indeed succeeded in their quest for financial freedom. But, their victory didn't come easy. It required the daily working of a true partnership. That partnership is not what we think of in a business sense. It is the partnership that evolves through marriage, founded upon true love and genuine friendship.

It is within the framework of family, holy matrimony, and hard work that Donna Fason reveals firsthand her remarkable story. Actually, it is also the story of every successful marriage because it reminds us that success requires a mutual commitment to become financially secure. She reveals her own travails that tempered her growth as a stronger, more self-assured person. By learning through trial and error, and educating herself, she became essential in her husband's network marketing business.

Words like inspirational, encouraging, and the like, don't do justice to this monumental work. Donna Fason hardly needs any words of praise as her pages are replete with her own words and revelations that will strike a chord in the heart of every reader.

Donna and Robert Fason are inseparable. As the song goes, "You can't have one without the other." Their love is radiant and everlasting. Her book is a mirror of who she is and who they are. I have had the great fortune of reviewing many books by many big-name authors over the years, and I have always kept an eye cocked for original thinking and provocative thoughts. That's the stuff that triggers our own imagination and brings us into worlds where our own dreams are born and on occasion can be realized. This is such a book. For those growing thousands upon thousands of Americans who are determined to be home-based entrepreneurs and are even more determined to achieve financial freedom, I unequivocally recommend that you read and reread Donna Fason's outstanding work product. You should take notes. You should underline. You should highlight. Even better, you should obtain copies for your own friends who are similarly situated and who share your own dreams. Give them a copy as a present. You will open up their eyes. They will be grateful.

There is a road called Financial Freedom that Donna Fason traveled. She chose to make the trip holding hands with Robert, her charismatic partner. The journey wasn't easy. It never is. But, there were pots of gold along the journey, and they continue their journey upward each day. Donna tells us her story — their story — in a remarkable way that assures us that we, too, can walk that same road and realize good fortune.

But only if we read and practice.

— Doc Lawrence
  Atlanta, Georgia

Wedding Picture
July 28, 1978

25th Wedding Anniversary

Preface

Hi, my name is Donna Fason; I'm from Mt. Vernon, Arkansas. I married my high school sweetheart, Robert Fason, over twenty-six years ago. We have two children: Joni, age twenty-two, and Cody, age sixteen. We both grew up in the area where we now live and both on dairy farms. After getting married right out of high school, we got into the dairy business ourselves. We managed to struggle through about six years of dairy farming before going broke and being forced to pitch a tent and auction off all of our cattle and equipment we had worked so hard for. Robert ended up back on a dairy, working for my dad, and I ended up working in a factory. We then spent a couple of years, Robert in sales and I as a secretary, for some friends of ours who owned their own business. During this time, we were introduced to direct sales and network marketing. We started out on a part-time basis just to earn an extra one hundred dollars a week. As it turned out, within a couple of years, we were earning more on a part-time basis with network marketing than we were making full time with both of us working. We reevaluated this new concept called "Network Marketing," and made a decision to make a five-year commitment to it and go full time. I am a mom first and when this decision was made, Cody was just a few months old, so we decided that Robert would work the business and I would stay at home and raise our children. So, for the past fifteen years, I have seen a lot and certainly learned a lot about supporting your spouse in network marketing.

Now that our children are older and because we finally succeeded and can now afford for both of us to travel, we work our network marketing business together as a team. We now travel all over the United States and share with people everywhere how to succeed in our business.

Network marketing is so different from the traditional way of business. I find that some people have a hard time grasping the concept and when they do, it is usually just one spouse who gets it. One spouse is excited and ready to go while the other spouse is not so excited and can't understand why the other is. The spouse who is not so excited is more concerned with the why instead of what has their spouse so excited. They see that something else is taking their spouse's free time, plus they may be having fun, and none of this has to do with them or their family. A wall goes up, a red flag, maybe a little bit of jealousy and the problems begin. Been there, done that!

I've started sharing my stories on how I learned to deal with understanding network marketing from a spouse's point of view. The company we are with has even produced a video and audio of one of my talks. I have people everywhere tell me, "I wished my spouse was here," or they say, "Thank you, you've really helped me to understand." People tell me, "Your tape really helped my spouse."

After months of this kind of response, I've realized I have so much more to give than time allows on stage. I decided to write this book in hopes of helping more people. After all, the concept of network marketing is people helping people. It's about making a difference in other people's lives.

If I can make a difference for you, then I have succeeded. If I can make a difference for you, then I can make a difference for someone else.

I dedicate this book to *you*, my readers. You make a difference—you are my inspiration!

Husband or wife or significant other, I give you *Spousal Support in Network Marketing*.

CHAPTER 1

What Is Network Marketing?

I'd rather have 1% of 100 people's efforts,
rather than 100% of my own.
— J. Paul Getty

I'm going to first describe, from a spouse's point of view, what network marketing appears to be. Then I'm going to share with you what it really is, once the blinders are down.

This was something that I struggled with for a few years. I was very unhappy and miserable because I just didn't understand nor did I want to understand. I saw network marketing as a threat to my marriage. It was a thing that took my husband away from our kids and me. It was something that took away any extra income from my family.

The jealousy that I felt from this thing called network marketing had me so miserable that I lost all self-esteem that I ever had. I was almost in a state of depression. I even lost the only thing that I thought nothing could ever take away from me and that was to be a mommy for my kids.

Kids are so innocent; they don't have a clue about life. I would find myself telling my daughter, "I would if I could" or "We can't afford it right now." At the same time, Robert would be spending money on gas or meals to do this thing called network marketing. I couldn't understand why we were doing without, while he was, what I thought at the time, having fun.

We had one decent vehicle and guess what? Robert had it all the time. If I did manage to land a job that would pay enough to cover day care for two kids, gas, lunch, and a decent wardrobe, I didn't even have a vehicle to get me there. Another issue was, Robert and I both made the commitment to do network marketing full time, so if I did get a job, what would that do for the network marketing business we had started? Robert was traveling, working full time, and sharing with people how to make a living in network marketing. His belief was so strong that we would succeed; my taking a job would not only destroy his credibility in our business, but him as well.

I had no control of anything. Network marketing was ruining my life; I didn't want any part of it. Since I wasn't involved and had no idea when or how much money I would have to spend on our kids, I couldn't tell them when we could go to McDonald's, or when I could take them to the zoo. I didn't have the answers they wanted to hear, so I felt I couldn't even be a mommy for my kids. I was totally helpless and useless. I hated what I thought network marketing had done to me.

Because I didn't *know* what network marketing was all about, I saw it as a thing that came between my husband and I. I saw it as one great big negative in my life. I will note though, I did figure out that being negative around people at our network marketing events was not a good thing. Robert and I had argued enough about this that I knew, when I had the opportunity to attend an event with him, I kept my mouth shut. I knew if I said something negative, he would probably not take me with him the next time. I enjoyed the times we were able to make trips together. We did get to spend time together and I desperately needed that time with him to realize that he did love me.

The more I started traveling with him, the more I learned about network marketing. Our business started growing and we were starting to succeed. Our roller-coaster income started to level out and then to grow each and every month. We were finally seeing the results of a four-and-a-half-year struggle.

We had finally made it to the top of the company we were with. When you are at the top, your name gets out; people want to know how you did it. We had become an overnight success in four and a half years.

There are literally thousands of network marketing companies out there and new ones starting up every day. Once we had succeeded and people knew who we were, people were calling us all the time, sending us videos and literature. They would say, "You made it with that company, you'll make a fortune with us." I have a whole file cabinet full of other deals, of which probably 90 percent are no longer in business. We glimpsed through the stuff but we were so happy that we were finally making money it was really hard to even think about doing anything else. We did, however, take a look at a company about seven years ago, and for several reasons we made the decision to resign from the company we were with and join our present company. We started part time and within thirty days decided to go full time. It has proven to be a wise and profitable decision for us.

The company, the product, and the pay plan are all major factors in your success with network marketing. But just as important, is *you*. Our claim to success where we are now is not that we were naturals; we paid our dues long before we ever knew about the company we're involved with now. I'll share some of those due-paying stories (of struggles and personal growth) with you later in this book.

Now, I want to share with you what I have learned — the real truth about network marketing.

Network Marketing is, simply put, people helping people to succeed in business. The concept of network marketing has been around for years. Let me give you an example: I go to a new restaurant; the food, the service, the atmosphere, everything, is great. I tell you about it and you go there. I have just networked you for that restaurant. It's sharing with others something good, kind of like a referral. The only difference is, that restaurant didn't send me any money for referring you, but by referring you to my network marketing business, when you buy or sell a product, the company does send me money. People network every day and don't even realize it. Maybe you tell someone about a great movie, a sale at a dress shop or whatever; you have just networked them. It's a pretty neat concept!

In network marketing companies, you usually have the company, the product, and a pay plan which explain how you earn money moving the products and helping others do the same. You will usually earn a direct sales commission for individual referrals or sales. You will then earn bonus commissions or overrides from referrals or sales made by the people who have joined you in your network marketing business. As your team grows with more people joining your team, so do your bonuses and overrides. It's all about people helping people to succeed.

To help you feel a little more comfortable with supporting your spouse in their business, ask your spouse these two questions. We've found these to be major factors in selecting a company and sharing it with our friends for long-term commitment and success:

1. Is the company over five years old?

2. Would I use the product if there were no money to be made?

I'm not saying that new companies won't succeed, but according to some studies done on this industry, not many will make it past the one- to two-year mark, but if they do make it past five, their chances of being here for the long haul are much greater. Fortunately, it has never happened to us — we've only been with two companies — but I have heard a lot of nightmares out there, where people have gotten involved and worked hard, only to find the company go out of business in less than two years. I see a lot of skepticism from folks because of this. The main thing is you need to feel good about what you are doing before you can share it with others.

My favorite part of network marketing is we have the opportunity to potentially earn above average incomes, without prior experience and without educational qualifications. That means everyone can do it, regardless of background and regardless of age, even a couple of ex-broke dairy farmers with only high school educations. *Wow!* What an opportunity!

The three key ingredients we're finding it takes to succeed are: a desire to succeed, a willingness to work, and being teachable. I've seen folks from all walks of life earning outrageous incomes in network marketing.

Everyone doesn't succeed, but don't knock it until you try it!

Here's our record with network marketing:

☐ The first four and a half years we earned just enough money to cover bare essential expenses.

- ☐ The next four years we averaged per month what we would have earned in a year in the dairy business.

- ☐ The next year we averaged per month what we would have earned in two years in the dairy business.

Our business is consistently growing; we now earn more per month than we would have earned in four years in the dairy business. You tell me, which would you rather do, milk cows for four years or work your network marketing business for one month?

I will admit, the first four and a half years weren't very pretty around my house and I wasn't very excited about network marketing, or very supportive. But, I can say now, after fifteen years and many, many, many dreams and goals becoming realities, my attitude and my involvement with network marketing has definitely changed.

CHAPTER 2

He's Not the Same Person I Once Knew

Until you make peace with who you are,
you'll never be content with what you have.
—Doris Morton

Do you ever feel like your spouse has changed due to their involvement in network marketing?

Do you ever wonder, "Where is the person I married?"

Do you ever feel like your relationship with your spouse has taken a turn for the worst?

Do your friends ever ask what's wrong with him or her?

Yes, to all the above! Boy did I!

Most of us are not so fortunate as to be rich when our spouses get involved with network marketing. That's usually the reason people get involved—to make money. I know that is why we got involved. We got involved, with my approval, to earn an extra one hundred dollars a week. I had no idea that I would have to go through the struggles that lay ahead.

With two small children at home and not enough money to afford baby-sitting and expenses of my tagging along, Robert went out to work our network marketing business. Out to work the business meant talking to people, sharing our products, and attending meetings. Our company used a weekly meeting as a way for people like us to bring our guest to hear someone more experienced with the business to share our opportunity. Plus, to better serve the masses, most of these meetings were held at night so people with jobs could attend and a lot of the time included dinner. They were either held in a restaurant or we were taught to offer our guest dinner to get them to the meeting. This didn't bother me too bad in the beginning, but then there came trainings and big events which usually were out of town and that meant gas money and hotel money, not to mention the fee for the training. Does any of this sound familiar?

Here I am, at home with two kids, and I don't have a clue as to what goes on at these so-called meetings and events. All I can see is my spouse is happy, having fun, eating at nice restaurants, and staying in nice hotels. People are calling my house for him all the time, and a lot of them are females whom I don't know, and now, I'm starting to feel a little bit jealous.

I did get the opportunity to attend a few of the big events and was greeted with, "Oh, so your Robert's wife," and I have to tell you, that didn't go over well either.

Our bills were piling up and I told my kids, "I would if I could," so many times it wasn't funny, and the only thing I could see with this thing called network marketing was that my husband was having the time of his life while our kids and I were doing without and miserable.

He refused to discuss any financial problems that we were having. If we ever started a conversation on money, it ended up an argument and he flat refused to discuss it. He would end the conversation with, "Don't worry about it, everything's great," and then leave the room to do something else.

Since I was the one at home, I had to answer the phone calls from the creditors. I had to beg the utility companies to give us a little longer. I was the one making the promises to pay, yet he was the one in control. Did I worry? All the time.

My self-esteem had gotten so low; I would stay in bed all day at times. I felt my husband had a new life now, which obviously didn't include me. I couldn't give my kids the answers they wanted to hear; it was all me, all my fault that my family was falling apart. I wasn't a good wife; we argued all the time. I wasn't a good mommy; I couldn't give my kids the things they wanted. I had no control over anything in my life. I was totally helpless and useless. I had finally hit bottom.

It was a normal day, as normal as it could be back then. Creditors calling all day, and me making promises I knew I couldn't keep. Then our daughter came home from school so excited about the upcoming school pageant. She said, "Mommy, can I please get in the pageant?" I had to try and explain to my little girl with tears in my eyes how expensive it was to get a dress; the entry fee and everything would be over one hundred dollars that I did not have, but I would if I could. With sadness in her eyes she replied, "It's OK, Mommy, I understand." This was more than I could handle. Something had to give somewhere, somehow. We had struggled like this for almost four years with this thing called network marketing and I was fed up. I didn't care what it took, when Robert got home that evening, he was going to listen and he was going to give me answers and not just another, "Don't worry, everything's great." I wanted to know the date that we were going to make it, when could I stop worrying. I could no longer handle the wishing—I needed to know when and I wanted answers now.

I watched him pull up in the driveway and I was ready to let him have it. He was not going to ignore the issue this time. He opened the door and stepped into the kitchen where I was waiting, all smiles as usual. I started in about the creditors, about the kids, how miserable I was, and I demanded answers, now! He did something that I had never dreamed he would do. We had been together since junior high school; it was always Robert and Donna or Donna and Robert. He looked me in the eye, put both hands on each side of his head like blinders on a horse, and said, "Baby, I love you, but if we're ever going to succeed, I can't listen to this negative." He then turned around, walked out the door, got back in the car and drove away. My husband had just walked out on me. I was speechless; I could not believe what had just happened. I was hurt deeply; separation or divorce was something we both had strongly believed was never an option for us. We were both against it for us, and had always agreed we'd get through no matter what. But, there I sat, he was gone, and I did nothing to try and stop him. Everything went through my mind: maybe he had found someone else; after all, he had been gone a lot lately. Maybe I drove him away because I had not been very supportive of him or his business. There I was, blaming me again.

The longer I sat and thought, I decided no, it wasn't my fault. Then I got angry. All I wanted was for him to listen to what I had to say for a change and he couldn't give me the courtesy of listening. So, then I sat alone and screamed, I yelled, I cried, I yelled some more, I cried some more, then I felt hurt again. My emotions were crazy, angry, sad, angry, sad, back and forth until I realized it was getting late and he wasn't back home. Was he coming back? I didn't know.

I decided to go lie down and try to figure out, What I am going to do now? I heard the car pull up and I then started trying to figure out, What is he thinking by now? Is he thinking, Maybe she's cooled down by now, or is he thinking, This is my house and I don't have to go anywhere, or what? Then my mind went to, I just want him to listen to me, but I am afraid if I say anything he may leave again and I know I don't want that. He walked into the bedroom, noticed that I was awake, but we didn't say a word to each other. He got into the bed and just like a man, went to sleep almost instantly. (I'm sure if you're a lady, you will agree with me how men can just go fast asleep as if nothing ever happened.) This stirred up an anger in me again, but I didn't say a word. I then grabbed the remote control; it was late at night, I couldn't sleep, and I couldn't concentrate, so I just flipped through the channels. As I flipped through the channels, something caught my eye—an infomercial with Anthony Robbins. I watched and listened. In the few events I had attended with Robert, all the speakers had taught us to listen to motivational tapes or read motivational books. I heard them say it, but assumed that they were talking to the people who were working the business, not me. This show was about motivation, but nothing about network marketing; yet he was talking to me. It was about becoming a better person. I was desperate to change. I did not like the person that I had become. I wrote down the phone number, slipped out of bed, went to the kitchen, got out my credit cards and called for available credit balances. I found one that I could use—our Discover card, which I proudly refer to now as my Recover card—had an available credit of $210. The program that was going to change my life was $179. They said it was a twenty-four-day program consisting of twelve tapes; I was to listen to one side per day and my life could change. It only took thirty minutes per day. They said whatever you want to change in your life, you can change with this program: you could have a better relationship with your spouse, become a better parent, lose weight, get physically fit, whatever you wanted, you could have it if you followed their program. In my mind, they said, "Donna Fason definitely needs this," so I ordered it.

As I was waiting for it to arrive I was thinking, I need to focus on what it is I want from this program. Improving my relationship with my spouse would mean both of us working at it; we still could just barely carry on a conversation without an argument, so I wasn't ready for that without his support. Plus, I would have to tell him that I had just spent almost two hundred dollars that we didn't have. A better parent — well, I still didn't have the answers that my kids wanted to hear; that too, would include Robert. So, I decided I could focus on losing weight and getting physically fit and no one would know what I was doing. If it worked, I could go through it again with another focus.

I anxiously awaited the arrival of my new program that was going to change my life. I was finally going to do something that I did have control over, and that was to lose weight. I already felt better, just knowing they were coming. On the day my tapes arrived, I was actually happy that Robert wasn't home. Now I wouldn't have to explain what I had ordered and why, and I could go ahead and get started right away.

I could feel a change in myself the very first day. It was like a weight had been lifted, there was light at the end of the tunnel. I could hardly wait each day for Robert to go work his business so I could take my class. Each day I learned more and more. I started realizing and finding the answers for all the things that had gone wrong. Robert had been listening to motivational tapes, like he had been taught. I had always thought they were to help him in his network marketing business, not to help him as a person.

Being your own boss and succeeding in network marketing does require a lot of belief in yourself; I just didn't realize it at the time. Each day I realized more and more what and why he did the things he did. I realized that I had become a negative for him and until his belief in himself was strong enough, he had to stay away from negatives. He had quit watching the TV, he had quit reading the paper, and he had quit running around with our friends. I thought he was so caught up in his business he didn't have time for any of this anymore. I also thought that he was becoming too good for us. He was a big shot network marketer, owned his own business, and was a big wig. Since I didn't work the business with him, I had plenty of time to watch TV and read the paper. And I desperately needed friends. I finally realized that this was why we couldn't communicate. I was continuing to be surrounded with negatives while he was surrounding himself with positives. They don't mix well. One will win over the other. I began to realize that he was only doing what he had to do and needed to do for us to ever get ahead in life and get out of the financial mess we had gotten into.

No, neither of us has totally gotten away from TV, the newspaper, or our friends. We have just learned how to use it as a positive in our lives. We still like to see a good movie and we like to see the weather on occasion when we're planning a trip, to know how to dress. We do like to see the paper when positive articles are written like our kids' names on the honor role list from school, ball games, et cetera. And yes, we are still friends with all of our old friends. We do still keep in touch. We have total respect for our friends, as they do us. We all have different dreams and goals. It was tough for a while but we all realize now what each of us wants in life, we understand the changes in our relationships, and we respect each other for who we are.

Your friends can be touchy about your relationships. Sometimes they feel the same way when your attitude changes to a more positive one, as I felt towards Robert's behavior. Just stay focused on your goals; true friends are still there! Our true friends never knocked what we were doing; they just strongly suggested that they couldn't do network marketing. Some of them have since joined us in our network marketing business and are going through some of the same things that we did. Even though our struggles were tough, the experiences have allowed us to help our friends through it a lot quicker and to see success a lot sooner.

If we had continued to hang around and listen to the suggestions of not being able to succeed, we would have soon seen ourselves as not being able to succeed. As hard as it seems to walk away with your blinders on, I can only imagine how hard that was for Robert to walk away from me, but that is what we have to do if we want things to change. Your friends may not understand at first, but just like me, they will later. I learned that you can't change someone else; you accept them for who they are and move on. The old saying, "It's OK if they don't buy your story as long as you don't buy theirs," really does say a lot. Once your belief in yourself is strong enough to overcome their objections, then you will succeed and you will find that your friends are still your friends.

We had to stop and think, We're in this business full time. We had to focus on what was right for us. If we wanted to succeed like the people we saw in the front of the room, we had to do what they were teaching us to do. If that meant spending a weekend at a training seminar instead of a weekend of leisure with our friends, then that's what we had to do. After all, neither of us had a job or education to fall back on for income. We had to develop a "whatever it takes" attitude.

I learned to set goals and to achieve them. I learned you can have what you want from life. Before long, Robert and I were talking without arguing. Our relationship was healing; things were finally changing in my life for the better. My life and my future looked so much brighter and all I did was listen to a thirty-minute tape each day. Yes, I did lose weight, and yes, I did become a better mommy. I was happy for a change!

I do want you to realize what happened to me—I changed my way of thinking. None of my circumstances changed, my kids still wanted, the bill collectors kept calling, and our business did not explode that very day. What I learned was to change my way of thinking on a daily basis. I had been looking for the answers to my problems in all the wrong places. My old thinking was, If the kids wouldn't ask for it, I wouldn't be upset that I couldn't give it to them. If the bill collectors wouldn't call, I wouldn't be angry that they had. And, if Robert would go ahead and get our business to take off, I would be disappointed each day when it didn't happen.

I began learning the process and the power of positive thinking. For things to change for me, I had to change. That's easy for me to say now, because I've lived it and I've survived it, and my family has survived it. But, remember it wasn't easy to get to this point.

If you're experiencing some similar thoughts and situations, how can I get you to understand how important reading motivational books are for you as a spouse? This was not taught to me in school and probably not to a lot of you; therefore, we don't realize how it can improve our lives on a daily basis. I was, however, excited to learn that our schools are now encouraging our kids in this area. I was at our children's school a couple of years ago and up on the bulletin board in the hall was a huge poster titled, "To Achieve Your Dreams, Remember Your ABC's." I had not seen this before and was so touched by it; I ran back to the car to grab a notepad and pen and wrote it all down. I've also been told from one of my nieces that every freshman entering one of the classes at a local college are required to read the book, *Tuesdays with Morey*. I do have that book and it is awesome and very motivational. We're also seeing a lot of this in the corporate world. Big-name motivational speakers are traveling the world to speak at seminars for corporate sales teams and leaders.

But how are you, a spouse, like I was several years ago, who has never been exposed to this, to know? All I can ask of you is to trust me and try it. I don't necessarily recommend one author over the other. I feel that is up to the person who is going to read the book. The key is to get a book in your hand and read it or a tape in your player and listen to it. I do have some books I prefer over others because I can relate more to them and understand them. I do enjoy inspirational books, as well as motivational. I have in my library of books and have read as well, almost every *Chicken Soup for the Soul* book. I have subscriptions to *Guideposts* and *Angels on Earth* and each time a new issue arrives, I sit down that night and read it before I go to bed.

Motivational and inspirational books tell true stories about people's lives. They help us to get through our own day-to-day struggles by sharing stories of how others got through their struggles. There are thousands of books out there—just start reading. I've learned that I wasn't the only person in the world to ever feel down and out.

Have you ever shared a story with a friend about your child misbehaving in public and how embarrassed you were and your friend came back with a similar story about their child? Even though you didn't feel better about your child's behavior, you did feel better knowing that your child wasn't the only one to do such a thing. Right? And, that you weren't the only person in the world to ever experience such an event. That's how these books and tapes can help you.

I knew that at one point in my life, I was happy; I was on top of the world from elementary to high school to graduating, getting married, starting our own business, and raising a family. Everything was going according to plan, I was moving on up with my life, and I was living my dreams! I don't know when, where, why, or how I ended up at the point that I did. Somewhere in the process of the responsibilities of running a household, managing a home-based business, and being a parent while struggling to get by financially, I quit dreaming. I started thinking survival instead of getting ahead in life. I didn't realize it then, but I certainly do know now, just how true Earl Nightingale's quote, "You become what you think about" really is.

We all have secrets in our lives, things that we struggle with by ourselves and that we tell ourselves will get better, but guess what? They don't get any better until we do something to make them better.

Our financial struggles were our business; they were our secret. I would die before I would let our parents and families and friends know how bad it really was. Our arguments were our business, our secret again; I wouldn't dare let anybody know there were problems in our house. I was already feeling failure enough and the last thing I wanted to hear was, "I told you so." Robert had approached some of these people with his network marketing business and they had laughed at him and blew him off.

Seeing that program on TV rather than at a business function, really hit home with me. It gave me hope and made me realize the importance of believing in me. It showed me how just a few minutes each day could change my life. Remember this folks, at that time in my life I wasn't anywhere near a network marketer, nor was I looking to become one. I just wanted to be happy again. I wanted answers to my problems.

I'm not telling you to read the books so you will join your spouse in their network marketing business. I'm telling you to read the books so you can understand where your spouse is coming from when they act like somebody you've never met.

Once you've tried reading the books, your belief in you will get stronger. It doesn't matter how strong we think we are. We need to be pumped up on a daily basis. Once you're reading the books, you will find yourself dreaming and thinking, What if ? You may even set some goals of your own and achieve them. And the next thing you know, you will be doing things you thought you'd never do.

You might find yourself wearing that outfit or suit that looks better on you than it did on the model. You might just go ahead and play basketball with the kids, something that you haven't done in years. And, if you're like most people who are really busy, you might just find yourself relaxing and enjoying that one-hour massage at the spa, because you deserve it! You might just find yourself waking up one morning saying, *"Wow,* isn't life *great!"*

I didn't read the books to get involved with network marketing. I read the books to feel better about myself, and to believe in myself again.

It was a few years later when I did begin to get interested in my husband's business. From what I had learned about personal growth and belief in myself, I started wanting to become involved in Robert's business with him.

It had been our business all along, I just never looked at it that way; but by now I knew this truly was our business.

Donna teaching a class on attitude

CHAPTER 3

Always Feel *Great!*

Dost thou love life? Then do not squander time,
for that is the stuff that life is made of.
—Benjamin Franklin

Once you've understood what it is your spouse is doing with network marketing and you've listened to something motivational to understand what positive thinking is all about, you will need to learn that no matter what, *always feel GREAT!*

I know that there's a time and a place for everything. I know life can't always be great, you will have bad days. People with positive attitudes do have bad days, we just don't see them. We think that they are always happy and everything is perfect for them. I felt that way about Robert before I understood the power of positive thinking. He never let me see him down and he never talked to me about his problems because he knew I was already about as low mentally as a person could get. He needed to feel better and in order to feel better he would go to events and meetings where people were positive and let it rub off on him.

I learned about feeling great from other spouses in our business that had more experience than I did. We were at a pretty big event and during one of the breaks I just asked another spouse, "How do you do it?" She asked me, "What?" I asked her, "How do you keep going and keep being so happy when you are the one home with the kids all day every day, you take all the phone calls, keep the house, the laundry, the cooking, the errands, the paperwork, ordering products and everything to do with your network marketing business and all your spouse does is run the roads, eat in nice restaurants, and have fun. How do you deal with that and yet feel great about it? I think we spouses are getting the wrong end of this deal!" Her reply to me was, "Donna, think about all the hours that Robert spends away from you and your kids. Think about all the ball games and fun stuff for your kids that he misses. Think about all the nights it's late, he's tired and still three hours away from home." She also said, "Donna, Robert wants to be home and spend time with you and the kids more, but if he intends to build any kind of a future for you and your family, he has to do whatever it takes now to build his business. To build and develop leaders with network marketing does require some traveling and training to teach others to duplicate your efforts. Once he has others trained to do what he does, he will be able to be home more and spend more time with your family."

I had to realize that as this was happening, our business was growing, we were helping others, and in return our income was growing to justify all the hard work that Robert was doing. His goal was not just to pay the bills, but to help enough other people get what they wanted so we as a family could have everything that we wanted. He was doing this for me and our kids to have a better future.

I got the opportunity a few weeks later to show him how I too could feel great!

Again, another normal day at the Fason house; Robert left early to go work his business with presentations all day, the last one being about three hours from home. I had just settled into my recliner to watch a movie about midnight and my phone rang. It was Robert, and the first thing out of his mouth was, "How was your day?" Remembering my conversation with the other spouse, that I needed to be supportive I said, "*Great!*" With surprise in his voice he came back with, "Really, what did you do today?"

At this time, Joni was ten years old and Cody was three. Here was my day and my answer:

I started with, "Well, we woke up around 9:00 a.m. and you know that stomach virus that's going around? Well, Cody has it. He woke up with a 103-degree temperature, vomiting and diarrhea every fifteen minutes. By the time I got one mess cleaned up, there we'd go again. That went on for several hours. And oh yeah, remember Joni went to a friend's house today for a slumber party? I got a phone call around 5:00 p.m. saying that they had all gone swimming and were riding in the back of a pickup truck, sitting on the tailgate with wet suits on and driving on a paved road. Joni slipped off of the tailgate onto the pavement and was skinned up pretty bad. They said I should come pick her up and take her to the emergency room. So, I called my sister to keep Cody while I went to get Joni. My sister made her husband, who runs from anyone sick, keep Cody so she could assist me with Joni. We got to the hospital; they ran X-rays, no broken bones. So, they sent us to the waiting room for four hours. We finally saw a doctor, he treated the scrapes like burns, wrapped her up like a mummy, and we went home. I got her settled, and then went to pick up Cody. By this time, he was much better, no fever, no more vomiting and diarrhea and I got him settled in bed. Then I kicked back in the recliner to relax and we've been home about fifteen minutes. But other than that, my day has been GREAT!

How was your day?" I then heard dead silence and I was thinking, Silly cell phones, we got disconnected and I've been rattling for five minutes to nobody. I said, "Hello, hello." Then finally I heard, "*Wow!* You did all of that and your day was great?" Again, with a very excited voice, I said, "Yes, how was your day?" Well, naturally he was going to say great, no matter how his day went. Most men, especially mine, would rather take a beating than to go through what I did that day. If I could still feel great after all that, even if his day had been terrible, he wouldn't admit it, so he said great too.

It's all in attitude. I finally understood what a positive attitude was all about. When those bad days happen, and they will, we do have a choice. We can have a bad day and continue to feel bad or we can have a bad day and end it feeling great. Either way, a bad day is a bad day. Personally, I like the great day!

I want you to try this sometime when things don't go as planned and you have a bad day: When you go to bed at night tell yourself, I feel *great!* I want you to really mean it. Forget about whatever happened, tomorrow is another day; just tell yourself, I feel great, over and over until you really do feel great. I promise, you will rest better, tomorrow will be a much better day, and you will be a happier person.

I hear this all the time and I've read it in several books: If whatever has upset me won't make a difference in one, five, or ten years from now, why let it bother me now? Blow it off and move on! Life is too short and too precious to not enjoy it.

I have a sign by my telephone in big letters that reads, "GREAT!" I keep it there to remind me how much that one word can make a difference in other people's lives. Here's a quick story on that: I'm not a real good morning person. One morning, I got up and walked to the kitchen half asleep, when my phone rang. I should know better than to answer the phone until I am fully awake, but I answered it anyway. It was someone in our network marketing business and they asked how I am doing. I answer with "I'm OK." Immediately, I heard the tone of the person's voice drop about three notches. People were so used to my *great* attitude, that to hear me any other way was a little discouraging. I felt bad because I realized that my attitude had changed that person's attitude. Just because I was sleepy was no reason to make someone else feel bad. That will never happen again.

Try using the word *great* in your vocabulary every day as much as possible. See what responses you get from people when you say, *"Great!"* Robert went through McDonald's one morning, and as with all customers, the girl at the window asked him how he was doing. His response was, of course, *"Great!"* She looked at him and a big smile came across her face as she said, "You don't have to work today, right?" He said yes, and as she handed him his order, she just kept smiling. She may have thought he was crazy but it sure put a smile on her face and brightened up her day. Tell a co-worker, "You look great!" Tell your children, "You did a great job!" Notice how much it raises their spirits. Try it on your spouse when he or she has just returned home from a meeting (and is really afraid of your response), but asks about your day anyway, just to start up a conversation. You will be surprised at how much closer your relationship can get with your spouse!

It didn't matter that at the time, I did not work our network marketing business with Robert. We could at least now carry on a conversation without an argument. We could communicate again. That was what I had wanted all along and now I understood how I could accomplish that. We could now start discussing our finances. We knew where each other was coming from and we began working together instead of against each other to make a plan to get us out of our mess.

I want you to think about this. All I did was change my attitude by adding the word *great!* And really meaning it. That one little word can change everything.

CHAPTER 4

Your Spouse Needs Your Support and You Need Theirs!

Give others a piece of your heart,
not a piece of your mind.
— Unknown

I'm sure you have days with the kids, whether at work or at home, that have been pretty stressful. By the day's end, it would help your feelings tremendously if your spouse would share a cup of coffee, relax on the sofa, or snuggle in the bed and reassure you that things will be OK and they will get better. We all go through it — we all have times when we need a shoulder to lean on — and the most comforting shoulder is that of a spouse. We need to feel loved and appreciated.

I had finally accepted the fact that Robert was going to do network marketing with me or without me. After discussing our finances and looking into the income possibilities, it did make sense. If he put the hours into network marketing that he would have to put into a job, he could make more money. The problem was, could he work for himself as the boss? I knew he was gone a lot and on the phone a lot. He always said he was working, but I couldn't tell it by the income.

After going through the motivational tapes, and the *great* attitude, and sharing with each other our day's events, it finally hit me! He would tell me things like: I talked to this person, or that person, and this is what they said. He would tell me who was at the meeting and what happened there. He was working the hours on his network marketing business. Why wasn't he making the money to compensate for the hours he was working? Network marketing is a numbers game. It's a people-helping-people business. He just hadn't talked to enough people yet to find the ones who wanted it. Little did we know, after four and a half years we were almost there!

We had worked for six months promoting a major event. Our sponsor had told us if we had twenty people there, our business would explode. Well, I was way past ready for that explosion, so I started doing what I could to help. We finally had twenty people make the commitment to go. We left late at night for our eight-hour drive so we could arrive the next morning for start time and save a hotel charge for one night. I was beginning to get excited; our business was going to explode! We registered for the event and began to look around for the twenty people who committed to coming. We couldn't find one person. We went ahead and sat in on the events, thinking, Maybe we just missed them, surely we'd run into them before the weekend was over. For two and a half days we searched through the crowds; still, no one. Not one of the twenty showed up. We were terribly disappointed and let down.

As we listened to the speakers and heard the stories from people ages eighteen to ninety that had only been in network marketing for six months or less and had already earned unreal amounts of money, we got more upset. I saw Robert was really down. I had never seen him like this. I got scared.

As we started our long drive home, he quit network marketing. He said, "I give up, I'm just not cut out for this. I've done everything I've been taught and it's just not working. I don't know what else to do."

I began to get really nervous about our future and I was trying to think of what to say to help. We began to discuss things we had learned from the event. One speaker said, "The only way you can lose is to quit. Don't ever quit!" Another speaker said, "You ain't gonna make it with the ones you got!" Obviously, not the ones we had! Then we discussed the success stories we had heard. Those people were no different than us; if they could do it, so could we!

I don't think anyone other than me as his spouse could have given him the support that he needed to continue on. I knew that a shoulder to lean on to vent his feelings from a bad weekend and a great attitude to support him and encourage him could get him back on track.

Ever since we had learned how to communicate again without arguments, we could also cheer each other up. He definitely needed some cheering up. I had enough belief in him and what he was doing to not want to let it go.

We discussed each other's feelings about the weekend and gave each other the strength and the confidence to succeed. We set a game plan and went to work.

Before we arrived back at home, we had a whole new list of names and a "nothing's gonna stop us now" attitude. We became a team, and one way or the other, we were going to succeed. Robert had worked too hard for too long to turn back now.

The very next month, things started to happen for us. Somebody knew somebody who knew somebody and some people turned up who wanted success as bad as we did. Our group did enough business to advance us to the next position with our company. After four and a half years of struggling we were finally earning money! Our income grew each month and we never looked back.

I'm so thankful that I was there with Robert. Had he quit, it would have been the worst mistake we ever made. We had no way of knowing our success was just around the corner. We would have never seen it happen!

Now, I want to share a story about how my spouse supported me at a time in my life when I so desperately needed it. On April 21, 2000, we were on our way home from our son's baseball game and we got a call on our mobile phone. It was our daughter informing us that my mom had just called and my dad was being rushed to the hospital; they thought he had had a stroke. Three days later, I along with six brothers and sisters, were called into a private room with a doctor. He had just finished talking with our mom. He was telling us what we already knew, but didn't want to face. Our daddy had gone into a coma, everything had totally shut down, and machines were all that were keeping him alive; he would not ever get better. We had to make a decision, the hardest decision any of us had ever had to make in our lives. This was the first time in my life to ever face losing someone so close to me.

Our business was exploding and growing and we had events and meetings scheduled daily. I could not do it! At this time in my life, I thanked God to be involved in the network marketing industry! With a traditional job, I would have been forced back to work much sooner; Robert just handled everything for me with our business.

Our daughter was graduating from high school in three weeks and we had guests coming in from out of town. Our houseboat was ready to be delivered the week after graduation. We had been sharing pictures of this boat with my daddy for almost a year. He was as excited about the boat as we were. Now, I was just "there," going through the motions, no help to anyone.

Suddenly, mom was in pain, and we took her to the emergency room for five hours waiting for an answer. We finally found out it was her gallbladder, and surgery was scheduled for the next day.

We had the christening ceremony planned on Memorial Day weekend with over eighty leaders from our company invited. Here I was. I had to plan and prepare food for all of these people. I did what I had to do to get through the weekend. Robert just kept comforting me and supporting me through it all, letting me take my time to pull myself back together. I was struggling with a lot on my mind all the time. Before I knew it, over two months had passed and I had done very little in our business. I felt like I was ready to get back to work, but had been so out of touch, I had no clue as to where to start to get involved again. It hit me at an event we hosted on our boat in June. We do a "Whatever It Takes" Workshop where we teach people in our business to work on themselves, more than on the actual business itself. One of Robert's comments was, "You can't stay positive and hang around negative." I know he probably meant it for the whole class but in my mind, he was talking to me. I wasn't hanging around negative; I was just staying away from the positive. I wasn't continuing to read or listen to positive books and tapes. I wasn't attending the events to hang around positive people. I thought about it and realized what I had been doing—I was missing out! If I ever needed a positive attitude in my life, now was definitely the time. I knew that if I was ever going to get back to being myself and doing the things I had done before with our business, I needed to be back around the people. That workshop is what got me back on track. I realized that nothing I could do could change anything that had happened in my life the prior two months; I wanted to be happy again and be a part of our business again.

I now realize that by continuing to read and listen to motivational materials, and even more so, to be around positive people, I can handle whatever happens in my life.

There are always going to be things happening in our lives, and as long as we can be there for each other, we can get through anything.

CHAPTER 5

Do You Ever Feel Like Your Spouse Has No Time for You and Your Family?

Every tomorrow has two handles. You can take hold
of the handle of anxiety or the handle of enthusiasm.
Upon your choice, so will be the day.
— Unknown

I feel like this quite often—even now after we have succeeded with network marketing and are making lots of money.

I blamed Robert's business in the beginning as the reason he was always too busy for us, but what now? A lot of the things my husband does with his free time has nothing to do with the business. He is really into elk hunting, deer hunting, turkey hunting, you name it—he loves to hunt.

Years ago, he always dreamed of going to Colorado to go elk hunting. He did not have the opportunity because we could not afford it then. Now that we can afford it, he goes every year and is living his dreams.

The biggest reason I have for still struggling with this issue is because for so long, while we struggled in the dairy business and then in network marketing, I became very dependent on him. I kept the house and the kids and only went grocery shopping when he gave me the money to. I would focus my spare time on things that: (1) cost nothing to do, (2) made little money, and (3) filled the empty hours in my life with something to do. I had a group of friends and we met one day a week. We clipped coupons and collected box tops and wrappers for mail-in rebates. We even went to the city dump to collect the box tops and wrappers. It would take the whole day; gathering, cutting, and sorting. I did save money and I got a few rebate checks. It was fun and rewarding for me then. I even helped the local grocery store owner stock shelves and clean one day a week, so in return I could cash in my coupons on things in the store for things that I needed. All of this did help out tremendously, considering the financial situation we were in at the time.

But now I think, Well, I can spend the whole day clipping, sorting, and gathering to save maybe one hundred dollars a month, or I can spend the whole day relaxing by the pool talking to people on the phone about our network marketing business and earn an unlimited amount of money. I have finally seen the big picture in network marketing and how it can change your life. I want more!

The reality has set in that, Hey, we have done it; we can live our dreams. Robert is living his dreams. He even works our business as he goes. He has people all over the country who have the same likes he does, and as he travels all over to help them with the business, they put him on a hunt of a lifetime.

I, on the other hand, didn't know for a while what I wanted to do. I had a lot of material things on my list of dreams, a lot of which I now have. But what did I want to do?

One thing I did a few years ago was learn to play golf. First, of course, with Robert, and for a long time I would not even go unless he could go too. But we finally had some friends join us in learning and I could go with them and still have fun. This did give me a little confidence in myself to do something that I liked without my spouse. It gave me a little feeling of independence as well.

I have liked spending a lot of time with our kids. We would go shopping and out to dinner. We'd ride go-carts or play putt-putt. But I realized they were growing up and had their own friends to do things with, so I found myself again wondering, What is it that I wanted?

I thank God for the people in our business who really want to succeed in network marketing, because they give my life a purpose. I love to help people. I love to see others succeed and get the things in life that they deserve. It's kind of like seeing your kids grow up and do a good job in school.

We can now afford for both of us to travel with our business so we do spend more time together now than we ever have. I love to travel! That was something that was unheard of in the dairy business. In the summertime, we take our kids and we all get to see new places together.

Our lives have changed so much over the years, and network marketing has given us the personal growth and the income to make changes in our lives.

I don't struggle too much anymore with what to do. I just do what I want to do. I can sleep in late, I can lay out by the pool, talk on the phone, go shopping—you name it—and I can do it. I don't wake up to an alarm reminding me it's time to go to work. Each day I think, *Wow!* I sometimes pinch myself to see if this is really real.

I am so glad that I got involved with my spouse and network marketing. It truly is an awesome lifestyle!

On our 3,000 sq. ft. houseboat with our leadership team

CHAPTER 6

Twenty-Four Hours a Day — Home Office

Yesterday is a cancelled check; tomorrow is a promissory note; today is the only cash you have, so spend it wisely.
— *Kay Lyons*

Since my husband and I have owned our own business most of our lives, this is something I have learned to deal with for years.

The thing that I like the most about working from my own home is being able to pick and choose my own hours to work around my kids and family schedules. I can be home when my kids arrive home from school. If they need me for anything, I can be at their school in less than five minutes.

I do have a separate room in my house that is strictly my office or at least where all of my office stuff is set up. Network marketing does require some phone work so we can talk on the phone wherever we are in the house or outside with a portable phone. I also like the fact that we can dress casual and comfortable for work.

Working from home and choosing your own hours does allow you the opportunity to sleep in if you like and take a break when you like. Remember though, with network marketing, you are your own boss and you generally get paid what you are worth; you do have to employ yourself. It's really easy to take a break in front of the television, get interested in a movie, and your "break" lasts for two to three hours—so be careful. It's also easy to get tied up in housework or yard work and forget you do have a business to run!

Probably the toughest adjustment occurs when you or your spouse (or both) take that step to go full time in network marketing. At this point you have been accustomed to going to work every day and then all of a sudden you don't have to answer to anyone but yourself. We tell ourselves, I'll make those calls later, and it feels good to sleep in for a change. You're also used to just one of you or both of you being out of the house all day—you've had a routine—and now it's all out of whack.

This does cause some tension with couples. One or the other messes the house up and doesn't clean up their mess. There are sometimes arguments over who did what and what was accomplished that day with your network marketing business. Sometimes our priorities get a little out of order. What you feel is important for your business may be totally opposite from what your spouse feels is important.

Before making the decision to go full time, sit down with your spouse and make a plan together. First, be sure you are financially ready. A lot of people struggle in the beginning. From my own experiences, struggling is not fun. You and your spouse decide together what is expected of each other. There may be parts of the network marketing business that you as a spouse can or want to handle. If you are working a job and your spouse is going to start working from home, let him or her know up front what you want to come home to. I know, if you are used to coming home from work to a clean house, you won't be happy when you walk in, and the place is a mess, and your spouse is taking a nap. Get all the details worked out and agreed on in advance. This way there will be no unhappy surprises.

When we decided to go full time in network marketing, I was already a stay-at-home mom. I've already shared some of our struggles with you. Basically, my duties were to take care of our kids, cook, clean the house, do laundry, and take messages. In the summer, I also took care of the outside chores of mowing the grass. I also handled the paperwork and the bookkeeping for our business.

After I had gone through the worst struggles and learned more about our business, I had become very excited about our opportunity but very scared to talk to anyone. I was so excited that Robert was willing to do that part of the business for us; I would gladly do everything else. As time passed and we were still struggling financially, the fights were on. I felt like I was keeping up my end of the deal and he wasn't. After all, my jobs were behind the scenes and never ending. I learned that talking to people is what makes you money in network marketing and since we weren't making money, I blamed him. I felt he wasn't doing his job. There were days when he didn't have appointments to go on or he didn't make calls, and he would lie on the couch and watch television, or take off and go fishing. I would get so angry, because regardless, I always had plenty to do. Our happy decision to go full time with network marketing was turning into an unhappy one; I was resentful in a big way.

Fortunately for us, things did get better. I had discovered the importance of believing in myself. Our love for each other gave us the strength to hold on through the tough times. Yours will too, as long as you are open and honest with each other.

Whether you work the business with your spouse or not, be a team player. If you will sit down together, and set your goals, lay out a game plan, and know what is going on, you won't be surprised when it is Tuesday night and your spouse has a meeting to attend.

A stop at the Royal Gorge on the way
to a Colorado ski trip with our kids

CHAPTER 7

Kids and Family and Network Marketing

*Nothing I've ever done has given me more joys
and rewards than being a father to my children.*
— Bill Cosby

This is a tough one! For anyone who has children, trying to juggle family and career can be tough. When I started working our network marketing business with my husband, I did start running into difficulties when it came to my kids.

I had always been able to attend special dinners at school and go on field trips with my kids. I'd always been there for them for just about everything they'd done.

Now that I'm traveling more with my spouse and participating full time with our business, I am faced with decisions over kids and career. The older our kids get, the more activities they become involved in. I find myself having to choose between business events and kid's events.

I am now as involved in our business as my spouse is. I am now one of the company's trainers and leaders. I now have responsibilities with our business and some events I can't possibly miss.

When I first started doing this, I was so excited to finally be a part of something. I could finally be me! I had come so far! But when my business events started running into my kids' schedules, I started feeling guilty.

I had finally found my purpose in life. I had over-come so much and I was so happy that I was helping others. I had finally become my own person. People knew me as me, not just Robert's wife, or Joni and Cody's mom. I was making a difference in other people's lives. People were coming to me for advice with their business — my self-esteem soared.

This all started during the summer while my kids were out of school and not quite so busy, so they traveled with us a lot. Then when school started back, their lives got really busy. They both are very active in clubs, organizations, and sports. I was faced with practices, games, and our business events; I felt torn down the middle.

I sat down with their schedules and my events, and updated my day planner. I then got the kids together and we discussed the importance of each event. We came up with a plan and a schedule for me where everyone was happy. There would always be that last-minute event or events that I did not have down that would conflict, but we would work it out.

I have to look at it sometimes as my job. With a real job, I know I would miss out on a lot more. Most days I am able to be at home when they come home from school. During holidays and summer break, we have a lot of time to do things together.

The flexibility of scheduling with network marketing has allowed me to be here for my kids. The personal growth that I have gained has made a huge impact on my kids. They have seen the changes in me; they hear and see positive attitudes on a daily basis. They have learned how to set goals and to achieve them. I feel like all the changes we have gone through have had a positive impact for my whole family.

I know which events are the most important for my kids and I never miss one. I feel very fortunate that the corporate leaders of our company believe that family comes first and they always understand when I have to miss an event to be with my kids. My kids also understand how important certain business events are for me and they support me.

I've only had one time when I had to make a major choice. Robert and I were to be promoted to the top position with our company, and on the same weekend, Cody was having his first part in a school play, a special school dinner, and his first judo competition. There will always be another event where I can be recognized, but never a first play and a first judo competition for Cody. It really wasn't even a decision at all; my priority was Cody.

Another thing we do with our kids that really helps them to understand why we do the things we do is: we all sit down—Mom, Dad, and kids—and set our goals. We ask each other, "What do we want from our business?" We plan vacations, fun things to do, things for the house, and outdoor fun stuff with the kids. We explain to them what we have to do in order to reach these goals, and then they understand completely when we have to miss a game or a practice. We also make a dream board where we have pictures of the things we want or goal cards with our goals written down where we can see it every day. This really helps when the kids ask, "Why is Daddy (or Mommy) always on the phone or gone to a meeting?" We can just look at our dream board with the kids and remind them why. Our dream board also keeps us motivated and focused on our business. We have our kids add some of their own dreams and goals as well. It gets pretty exciting around my house when someone gets to mark "achieved" on that goal!

I believe all the motivational materials our kids have been exposed to because of our business has made a difference for all of us.

Some people see network marketing as a negative when it comes to kids. I hear things like, "I can't go because I have the kids." I just go on to the next person because I know if I had a real job and a real boss, I would be missing a lot of my kids' lives. At least I know I do have a choice.

I feel network marketing has been the best thing ever for me and my family. Everything we've done in the past would never have allowed us the quality time that we now have with our kids. The trips we've taken together as a family while working our business are full of wonderful memories that will stay with us forever. Speaking of special moments with your kids and family—I want to share just a few. I want to start with a few stories about our kids.

Before we started making money, each year when it came time to buy school clothes, I would just get out the J.C. Penney's catalog and select what I felt was necessary. I did this because I knew what we could and couldn't afford and I could pay it out monthly. I didn't want to say again, "Honey, we can't afford that." Once the order came in, the kids were surprised and happy because they had something new. For years, my kids went to school telling their friends that their new clothes came from UPS. One day a couple of years ago, it was that time of year again and I decided to take the kids shopping for school clothes; after all, we could now afford whatever they selected. We made a whole day of it—what a great day! We had gone from one store to the next, shopping and buying. We had just left the shoe store where both kids selected two pair of shoes each and had carried them to the car so our hands were free for the next store. As we started back to the next store all three of us holding hands, laughing and talking, Cody, our son, just stopped.

He looked up at the store and knew this one particular name brand of jeans were in that store that he really wanted. He knew they were expensive, and looked up at me and said, "Mom, can we go in here and get some of those jeans?" I had a flashback of the times when I used to have to say, "We would if we could," and realized we could now. So I said, "You bet we can." He just stared and said, "Mom, I'm so glad you and Dad found that business where we can now afford this stuff!" I know we don't want to spoil our kids totally rotten, but I must admit it sure felt good to be able to do that and know that I could afford it.

Our daughter's last prom was coming up in three months. We had had some bad weather and school was closed for the day because a lot of our back roads were still covered with snow. We were sitting around deciding what to do for the day. Somehow the suggestion came up that we just load up and go shopping in Little Rock. Joni had wanted a pink prom dress for three years and every year we goofed around and didn't shop early enough to find one that she liked. This time we had plenty of time, so we went shopping and found the perfect one. This was her senior prom and we could literally afford any dress in the store; I didn't even look at price tags, I just wrote the check. I was so excited that we were in a position financially to be able to do that for our daughter for such a special occasion.

Some time during the spring of the same school year, our son came home from school with a brochure on Michael Jordan's basketball camp in Chicago. I didn't even know there was such a thing—we do live in Arkansas. He started begging to go. I knew how busy we already were with our business and that the company was planning a big event around the same time. We were expected to attend, but the exact date and location had not been announced. As it turned out, the event was the same weekend and it was in Chicago. *Wow!* Yes, he attended Michael Jordan's basketball camp and had an awesome time!

Now, I want to share a couple of stories about our parents and our dream board.

Each year, we write and post our goals and dreams. We don't always know how these will get achieved, but we do know they will never be achieved if we don't write them down. What happens is, we see them every day and our subconscious mind goes to work on ways to achieve them. At the beginning of 1999, we set a goal to get my mom a new car by the end of the year. Her car was eight years old and had a lot of miles and was beginning to have a lot of problems. We didn't buy the car, but her boss did give her one for Christmas that year.

I had found this out early in December, so I went to work on something else for her. In the company we are with, I can save a lot of money on jewelry, so I suggested to Daddy that he buy her a ring and I would get it for him to give to her. I knew she wanted it bad and had already picked it out and had planned on getting it for herself. I had to tell little white lies, like they didn't have it but would keep looking and maybe have it for Christmas. On Christmas day we always let the kids and grandkids open gifts first, and Mom and Daddy have to wait so we can all see what they open. We set the stage with the song, "Still the One," as my mom opened this present from my dad. It was the most beautiful moment and the best Christmas ever! We had no way of knowing that this would be the last Christmas with our dad. I know that God knew and made things happen the way they did so that my family could have that memory. It's not always about what we can or cannot afford or how much money we make or don't make. It's about being in the right place at the right time and making a difference in other people's lives. My dad was not the type of person to openly show his love, even though he was mellowing as he got older. He also didn't believe in spending much on gifts; he usually gave me a much smaller budget. I'm so thankful that he agreed with my plan. The memories of that Christmas are so special to my whole family, especially for my mom.

Another goal we had posted on our board was to get a new house for my mother-in-law. One of Robert's three sisters was very active with us in business and we discussed this a lot. She called me one day in late November after she had returned from shopping with their other two sisters. She said, "You won't believe it, we're buying Mom a house for Christmas." It turned out that the other two sisters had the same dream we did. So the four of them went shopping and handed my mother-in-law the keys to her brand-new house on Christmas Eve 1999.

Network marketing has not just changed our income — it has changed our lives in many ways. We have been able to see so many dreams come true for so many people. It's just a good feeling when you see that something you did or said made a difference for somebody else.

Our dreams and goals get bigger every day, and we know, because of what we've learned from this industry, that we will reach them.

Donna on our farm with some of our horses

CHAPTER 8

I'm Happy Where I Am . . .
I Don't Want Any Part of Network Marketing!

*You can't help someone get up a hill
without getting closer to the top yourself.*
— Gen. H. Norman Schwarzkoff

I hear this a lot. It's OK if you want to continue on in the career you have chosen. No one expects you to quit what you are doing to follow your spouse's dreams. You are your own person and you have your own dreams and goals in life. I would have never become supportive and gotten involved, just for my spouse to go hunting and nothing for me. I had to figure out what I wanted.

As I've already shared, in the beginning I was down and out, financially and emotionally. Network marketing was a big negative in my life. I probably would have been better off if I did have a job or a career because it would have given me something to do besides worry.

As time went by and things started happening with my spouse's business and he was succeeding, he did try to include me with his business and I rejected it. I had what network marketers call "I.T.C. syndrome," better known as the "I'm too cool syndrome." I had sat back and listened to so many people make fun of what my spouse was doing, I was totally ignoring his success. I was believing them instead of him. I heard: "He's a born salesman, he can do that but we can't"; "When is he going to get a real job?"; "When is he going to wake up from his dream world and come back to reality with us?"; "That kind of success doesn't happen in the real world." Since I didn't have a clue as to what network marketing was all about, I didn't have any comeback for the things I was hearing.

I found myself wanting to believe, but wouldn't let myself. After all, someone had to be logical and responsible; we did have a family to think about. I couldn't let myself in his dream world — we couldn't live our future on dreams! I even checked the want ads on a regular basis for some kind of a job, just in case. Having a job meant security for our future.

I did have living proof that the products we were marketing worked, and proof that the pay structure worked; we were receiving checks and they cashed. The company had been in business for several years, I knew it was here to stay; but yet, I could barely mention what Robert was doing and I got shot down quick. I was buying everyone else's stories. I was buying the traditional way of thinking — only people who get lucky succeed. Everyone had me believing that Robert was just plain lucky. They would say, "Ever since I've known him he could fall into a pile of cow manure and come out smelling like a rose." I had heard someone say that about Robert long before we ever saw network marketing, so I was believing them. I had finally come to the conclusion that the people I knew had normal lives and were happy, and I was not going to tell them they could live their dreams with this thing called network marketing. They knew and I knew that Robert's success was from luck.

I was perfectly happy that he was so lucky, after all, my bills were now being paid and I didn't have to worry anymore. I began to realize that his dreams were coming true, luck or no luck; there was definitely some-thing real here.

I did become more involved to see what this network marketing thing was, to see if it could possibly help me to have some of the things in my dreams. I started attending events and learning the business. Nothing was forced on me; I participated at my own pace. I did get to know the people involved, from the corporate level to the leaders in the field to the brand-new distributors. One thing I realized is that they were all normal people just like you and me. I realized they all had dreams and goals and were not only going for them — a lot of them were achieving them with network marketing. It wasn't just Robert being lucky. You talk about rags-to-riches stories; I heard a lot of them! I also met a lot of professionals like doctors, lawyers, and busi-ness owners who had actually changed careers to do this network marketing business full time. I was amazed at the success stories and the people from all walks of life. There were people from high school dropouts to college graduates to millionaires getting involved. And what was so strange is that it didn't matter; everyone had the same opportunity to succeed regardless of background.

I had heard my whole life how important a college education was so you could get a higher paying job. I had plans of getting married and going into the dairy farming business when I graduated from high school, and I didn't think that I needed a college degree for that so I never went. After going through our struggles and going broke in the dairy business and then our struggles with network marketing, I still believed that something better and something real would come along. I had already lost out on a college degree but something was out there. While still hoping and searching, I continued to support Robert by attending events. I began to realize, This thing is real! These people are real people! The more I was around it, the more I liked it and the more I believed in it. What happened was, I was now surrounding myself with positive people and not getting bogged down with the negatives.

I started getting involved with our business and focusing on the "what-ifs" and "what if we can succeed" kind of things and staying away from the negatives. What used to be Robert's dream world was now becoming our dream world. I liked what was happening. There were a lot of changes taking place in our lives. We were now doing things we had only dreamed of before. I was reading books and listening to motivational tapes constantly. I had a better attitude towards life. Our kids were happy, we were happy, and I no longer cared if other people laughed at us. I knew there were plenty of other people out there, just like us, and our job was to find them and to help them realize their dreams.

I look back at where we were and where we are now, and I know that network marketing has changed our lives. I try not to brag; I don't want to come across as conceited because I'm not. It's public knowledge what a lot of college-degree jobs are paying, and I see our monthly checks total more than a lot of college-degree yearly salaries. I have to ask myself why. Let me remind you, neither of us went to college. I have learned enough to know that I can't dwell on the ones who don't see it or want it; I focus on the ones who do and help them to succeed.

I'm not asking you as a spouse to forget your dreams and goals. I'm asking you to open your mind so you too can learn to be supportive as much or as little as you can. It just might be the encouragement your spouse needs to succeed.

I know a lot of people who are working and succeeding with network marketing and I have never met their spouse. They tell me their spouse does this or that and wants no part of the business, but he or she supports them in what they do. They have taken the time to share with their spouse what they are doing, how they are doing it, and why. They have explained their business, shown a video, or have taken their spouse to an event. They have given their spouse the opportunity to hear from others in their business. They have also sat down with their spouse and set goals together. They have shared with their spouse their plan of action: what, when, and where they are and where they are going with their business. By doing this, there are no surprises and negatives. They then continue to communicate with their spouse on their progress. It's no different than sitting down to dinner and discussing each other's day at work.

I've learned to ask questions and to be open with my feelings. If I feel my spouse is spending too much time with a certain group of people and nothing is happening with the business, I simply ask what is going on, and why that part of our business is not growing. I suggest that from what I've seen and heard on network marketing, it may be time to move on and say, "Next." Sometimes people get so caught up in wanting it more for someone else than that person wants it for themselves, they fail to see that they are the only one working. Whether we're a partner with our spouse or not, it does help to know how the business works so we can give them the encouragement they need when they need it.

All network marketing companies offer a product. If we have thoroughly researched the program and we feel the product has value, why not use it? This is another way we can be supportive without actually working the business.

A lot of companies have conference calls, fax on demand, Internet sites, and literature that all give us information about their products, company, pay plans, and events. By taking a little time to study the information, you can learn a lot about your spouse's business. Just knowing that you care enough to learn what it is all about, may be the support and encouragement your spouse needs. This was another thing that helped me to be supportive without actually working the business. I could at least answer a question when someone called.

I was a very negative person in the beginning because I didn't know what it was all about; I didn't understand the whole concept. I was so bogged down with negatives of my own, I didn't want to listen to the details and the process. I just wanted to know when I was going to have the answers for my problems. I had a "forget the details, just show me the money, honey" attitude.

After I started listening to motivational tapes and reading books, which again had nothing to do with working the business, I understood why he persisted with his dreams and goals. I became more open-minded to what he was doing. This was what he had chosen to use as his vehicle to reach his goals. He had already proven to me that my negative attitude was not going to stop him.

Now, I'm not suggesting that those of you doing a network marketing business bully up and do it regardless of your spouse's opinion; nor am I suggesting that you as a spouse feel like I'm saying you are wrong and your spouse is right. I am saying, together you can reach a happy medium.

I have also seen some people's relationships in network marketing turn sour. The blame usually goes to the network marketing business. I think that is just an excuse for a way out.

Success in network marketing does in most cases require support and communication from both spouses. If you are the one working the business, then treat it like a business and not a hobby. Be serious when you set your goals and make it happen. Spend your time wisely and effectively. It's much easier for a negative spouse to take a second look if they can see some progress.

I started learning and understanding what my spouse's business was about, and even though I wasn't out in the field with him, I did learn little ways of helping out. Rather than just take a message, I was able to answer questions from new people in our business. This allowed my spouse more time to work his business and to spend with our family, rather than spend that time returning phone calls. I learned how to fill out applications, place orders, and read reports. I knew when and where the events were so I could also pass that on when people called. I started handling the behind-the-scenes stuff so he could have more time to talk to people. Everything that I did was done from my home, and at my convenience, around my schedule. This did give me something to do with my spare time, plus it made me feel needed and useful to our business. It made me feel a part of something and good about myself again.

I know that you probably love what you are now doing and want no part of your spouse's business. That's certainly all right and OK to feel that way. I will ask you, though, to allow your spouse to share with you what their business is all about and get your questions answered. See what it is that has them so excited. This way you will know what is going on and know what you're up against. You will run into conflicts, and knowing what your spouse's business is about will help you to better understand, so hopefully your conflicts will be discussions instead of arguments.

After you've learned about your spouse's business, let your spouse know your feelings. For or against, let them know where you stand with their business.

You are a team in marriage and a team for life; we want to keep it that way. Just always be open and honest with your feelings and together you will survive.

CHAPTER 9

Maybe I Might Want to Do That Too!

Dream it! See it! Believe it! Achieve it!
You miss 100 percent of the shots you never take!
— Wayne Gretzky

Robert and I had already become successful and were earning a lot of money when I decided that I wanted to do what he was doing. I was already a partner with him in the business, a silent partner. Like I said earlier, I was known as "Oh, so you're Robert's wife." I was really working hard; our business had grown. I was doing all of the "manual" work. Besides my responsibilities as a mom, a wife, a maid, laundry lady, and kid's taxi, I was handling all the paperwork, bookkeeping, and scheduling events. At the events I did all the decorating, loading and unloading of products, setting up of the displays, and ran the registration table. It finally hit me one day that I was doing all the hard stuff and all Robert was doing was showing up, shaking hands, and talking to people. Robert always seemed so relaxed, just visiting and meeting new people. I was always stressing and running around like a chicken with my head cut off making sure everything was done.

I had become a true believer in our products, and we were making a lot of money. I had met the corporate leaders, so I did believe in the company. I was reading motivational books constantly and I did believe in me.

My problem was that I felt like everyone expected me to be as good in front of the room as Robert, because I had been there the whole time he had been involved with network marketing. I was always in his life, but not always in his business. By this time, I knew as much about the business as he did, I had just never shared my knowledge in front of the room. I watched Robert go through stage fright in the beginning, and he persisted until he was totally comfortable and relaxed as if he had done this his whole life. I knew, too, that I would have to stumble through until I was comfortable. Again, one major problem: I was scared to death of public speaking. I had finally made up my mind that I could do it, and I did manage to stumble and stutter through a couple of small speaking parts for our company.

Every time a new product was released, I'd think, Here's my chance to start! Then I would chicken out. After every big event or training, I would get all motivated and tell myself again, Here's my chance, only to chicken out again.

Remember, what sells in network marketing are the stories. Sure the product, the pay, and the company have to be good but the stories are what sells. The old saying goes, "Facts tell, but stories sell." We always teach people to develop a story. What makes a new person join is the stories they hear, the stories that they can relate to; maybe someone with the same background or someone they know. It's someone's story that helps them to see themselves doing this. I would attend the events and hear those stories, and get excited all over again, then go home and chicken out.

What finally made me realize that I had to do it — that no matter how scared I was, I had to speak — was the people. At the events, our one-on-one conversations during the breaks showed me that they had the same fear as I had. They were very inspiring! I knew everything about our business. I could answer any questions that anyone had. I found that the one thing we had in common was the fear of public speaking. I knew if I could overcome that fear, so could a lot of others. My doing so would not only change *my* life, but would change the lives of others. My desire to make a difference for others became so strong, I would not let myself chicken out. I accepted the fact that I would not be all that great the first time up and I would learn from my mistakes, but the main thing was *to do it*. I stuttered through, and each time it got easier. People now tell me how they can relate to what I say and that I helped them or inspired them to move on with their business. If they only knew what they had done for me! Knowing that I've made a difference in other people's lives has been the most wonderful reward of all. It's been worth whatever nervousness I've had to go through.

Since I have begun to work *every* aspect of the business with Robert, I have learned something: Our business is growing twice as fast and we are able to help twice as many people! What a concept! I love it!

Golfing in Cozumel, Mexico

CHAPTER 10

Having Fun!

You're only going to live life once, enjoy it while you can!
— Joe Lasley, my daddy

I never dreamed that I could have so much fun and get paid for it!

As I told you earlier, network marketing is basically people helping people. Robert and I and our kids have had the opportunity to travel and meet a lot of really neat and fun people. We've been able to see a lot of neat places, and stay at a lot of beautiful resorts and hotels — talk about fine dining, *wow!*

Let me share some of our experiences:

We took our kids to Chicago to do a big event with a couple who were our friends. They had joined us in our network marketing company and had a couple of extra days to stay and see the town. We toured the John Hancock building, and after that, wow, was I surprised! Did you know Chicago has a beach? Before that trip, I thought all the beaches were in Florida. We walked the navy pier, taking in the rides, restaurants, and fun. We ate pizza at the most famous — and first — pizza restaurant in Chicago called Uno's Pizza. You won't find pizza like that in Arkansas! This was a very educational and exciting trip for the whole family.

Robert and I went to Orlando, Florida, for a convention and the hotel had a restaurant that served the actual *Titanic* dinner. They had an original menu and put together a dinner just like it. It was wonderful! I can't say that I've ever had the salad after the main entrée before; again, a totally new experience for me.

We've had the opportunity to share so many things with our kids because of our network marketing business. They've had the opportunity to meet kids from other states, and develop friendships with kids they would have never known. There are occasions when we don't have time to explore the event city, but the kids still have a blast. They go swimming, watch television, and order room service. To our family, staying in a hotel is a vacation. We don't have to cook and wash dishes, we don't have to make our beds or clean our room. We really like that!

Together as a family, we've played in the ocean several times, been up in the arch in St. Louis, and watched a Cardinal's ball game when Mark McGuire hit two of his record home-run hits. We've been to Six Flags in Texas and in St. Louis. We've been to Disney World, taken a ride in a limo, gone on a boat ride in Lake Michigan, and deep sea fishing in the ocean. We've traveled to Branson, Missouri, several times. We have been able to do so much with our kids! And Robert and I get a lot of weekend getaways together as well!

Everywhere we go we work our business and meet new people; it's a pretty awesome lifestyle! We enjoy the travel; after all, we're two ex-broke dairy farmers, who never had the opportunity to leave the farm if we couldn't get back before the evening milking.

We've been on five Caribbean cruises as rewards from our company, but most of our travels have been within the United States because that is where our business is. We are now planning a vacation in Europe this year with our son, Cody.

As we travel, all the beautiful places to see and all the fun things to do amaze me. Sometimes people ask us if travel is required to work this business. We travel because we choose to. At times, we probably get more relaxation while traveling than we do at home. It is not a requirement, but it does help in building your business; especially if you want your business to expand into other states.

We met a couple through our business who have come to be dear friends. They live in a beautiful log home on a mountaintop near Eureka Springs, Arkansas. We sometimes go stay with them for a few days at a time so the guys can hunt, and the girls can shop—and in between we work our business over the phone. You talk about relaxing; the view from their home is absolutely gorgeous!

We met another couple from Florida who took us to the most beautiful park, located on the Rainbow River near their home. That river is crystal clear; we even went on a float trip while we were there. We went with a whole group of people in our business and had a blast!

We met another couple from Louisiana that we worked with for a couple of days. We had a company event at night for two nights and our days were free. The guys went fishing and the wife took me for a tour of the town. This is where I ate my first meat pie and dirty rice; it was different, but good. The town was an old historic one with brick streets alongside a river. It was really neat and interesting!

We spent another weekend with some people in Oklahoma, and I stayed in my first bed-and-breakfast. It was a very old historic house with lots of antiques. It's funny how these sorts of things "wow" us as we get older. While growing up in school, we sometimes think history is useless and can't wait for the bell to ring.

We usually try to schedule our travels so we can spend time away from the event with the people. We like to get to know the people in our business, to find out what it is they want from it, and how we can help. We like to get to know them better so they feel more comfortable with us helping them. We may have a barbecue before a meeting, or go to someone's house after a meeting, just to relax and visit.

Whatever we do, we find one thing in common everywhere we go. We find real people, who have dreams and goals, and who want more from life. I didn't know that I could feel at home in so many places. We have met some of the best people through network marketing. The friendships we have built are the greatest! The hospitality we have been shown is second to none!

For people who can't or don't want to travel, this type of business can be worked from your home: over the phone, through the Internet, direct mail, et cetera. Check out your options with your company. I do spend a lot of time in my summer office, which is a swimming pool in my yard. I relax by the pool, get a tan, talk on the phone, and make money! *Wow!*

Five years ago, we spent two days in Somerset, Kentucky, picking out and custom designing our new 18 ft. x 80 ft. Somerset houseboat. We designed the whole thing ourselves from the floor plans to the flooring, furniture, colors, and fabrics for the window covers and beds. We decided on four bedrooms and two baths with a large living room and kitchen area. The rooftop deck has a flybridge where it can be operated from the top of the boat as well as from the helm. We put a rooftop cover at the front of the upper deck with the back open for suntanning. We added a slide off of the back for the kids. We took delivery on that new boat in May, 2000 and wow, have we had a blast with it! We regularly take people out on it for a sunset cruise and show them our business. We've carried groups of as many as 130 people. We have had several training events on the boat as well. We designed a workshop for people in our business where they can come to Arkansas, spend some time on our boat, and learn how to build a big business. We call it the "Whatever It Takes" workshop. A local restaurant supplies meals and meeting space, and the local hotels accommodate our overnight guests. We spend about an hour after dinner in the meeting room and wrap up the first night with a cruise across the lake. The next day is spent in the workshop classroom, then it's back to the boat for fun, hamburgers, and working the phones for the business. We try to get about five or six of these workshops in before the summer season ends. It has proven to make a difference in the people who have attended; I've seen many people overcome their fears during these workshops. Once we get out on the lake, I've seen people who could not swim and were afraid of the water, jump in! I've also seen people jump off of the top of the boat when they had a fear of heights. I've seen many people conquer their fear of picking up the telephone. Once they recognize some of these fears and overcome them, they realize they can do whatever it takes to succeed in this industry. The group setting makes a difference because people realize others are overcoming their fears, too.

We do have to leave the boat a few times during the summer to travel across the country for company events. During the summer months, our two kids usually travel with us. That's why it worked out so perfectly for Cody to go to Michael Jordan's basketball camp; he was going to Chicago anyway! We had met a couple who joined our business about five years ago who have two kids close to the same age as ours. We went early to spend some time with them and work our business. They recently built their dream home and it is absolutely beautiful! We spent the day sunning on the back deck, talking on the phone, and working our business. The guys went four-wheeler riding, fishing, swimming, and played games. They had a blast! The girls went shopping at the mall. We had a wonderful barbeque and wrapped the evening up with an awesome business meeting with their local people.

Probably one of the biggest blessings we've had in spending time with people is the opportunity to get to know my sister and brother-in-law. Robert's sister, Rita, and her husband, Donnie, joined us in business seven years ago and have done quite well. I've had the opportunity to watch them grow with their dreams. We've spent a lot of time together, not just working, but having fun as well. We've traveled all over the country together attending events and having a blast. Our relationship has become much closer than ever before. It's more like we're best friends, rather than family. We share the same dreams and goals, and helping each other achieve them is one of the best parts of this business. It truly is awesome to see others succeed but it really is special when it's family. We now spend days together other than family reunions and special holidays. It's great!

I have people ask me all the time how many hours I work per week. I honestly don't know; when you're having fun, it's not work! All I know is, we just keep doing everything I've shared with you and every week we get checks in our mailbox. It doesn't get any better than that!

Afterword

Whatever your doubts or fears, I hope this book has helped. I know I haven't experienced everything, but I have seen a lot. I don't claim to have all the answers. Remember, whatever it is you're going through, someone else is going through it too. Talk to people; they can help you!

You will find yourself in a lot of the situations that I have shared with you. Understand that when you do, you will have to live it, experience it, and grow from it. You will survive it.

No one starts out in network marketing and makes it to the top without some struggles. Your spouse will struggle, and you will struggle in totally different ways. Your spouse will have others in their business to encourage them and help them and you will probably feel all alone. Just remember, *you are not alone.* If I've learned one thing from sharing my stories, it's that there are a lot of spouses in this business who have the same doubts and struggles that I have.

If your struggles are like any of mine, I hope my stories will help you get through them with a little less pain.

I wish you all the happiness in the world and may all your dreams come true!

At Greers Ferry Lake overlooking our houseboat *Whatever It Takes*

Aerial view of the over 1,000 acres we just purchased on
the lake where we will be building our dream home

Author Contact Information

Robert and Donna reside in Mount Vernon, Arkansas
with their two children, Joni and Cody.

Visit their Web site at:
www.bign.com/rfason

Or contact them at:

Whatever It Takes, Inc.
1004 Hwy. 36
Mount Vernon, AR 72111

Phone: (501) 849-2586
E-mail: robfason@aol.com

Notes

.

Notes

Notes

Notes

Notes

Notes

Notes

Notes

Notes

Notes

Notes

Notes

Notes

Notes

Printed in the United States
62668LVS00002B/2

9 781932 503388